1

Dear Ex

Bianca Perrie

For all the broken hearts out there.

I

Dear Ex,

Today,

I composed a list

of all the things

that I have wanted

to say to you

since the day

we broke up…

Number One: I Want You Back.

There was something about

the way you came to me,

and the way we came to be

(in the first place) –

I had wanted you,

before I got you –

like digging and striking gold.

I had wanted you,

so badly,

I probably willed you

to want to have me.

The way we were

drawn to one another

was moths to flame,

bats to caves.

It was a necessity,

an undeniable,

inexplicable

necessity.

I had wanted you

and then I got you,

and it's hard to say

who really chased who.

Want like ours

was two cats and no mice.

Want like ours

manifested paradise.

You ran for me

and I ran away…

until I ran toward you

and you did the same.

And it happened so fast.

We collided so fast.

You became mine so fast.

So, this want…

The want that I

have for you

is a selfish want.

I am a whole person without you,

but somehow,

your absence has made me feel

like a fraction of myself.

I am divided on this.

We broke up, so…

we must belong apart.

But I don't know

how I'm supposed to

carry on living

with this shattered, useless heart.

If I subtract the pain,

and carry the two,

the totality of the situation is

that I still want you.

Back.

I want you back.

I am a whole person without you,

but somehow,

you were sustenance to my soul.

Before I knew you,

I assumed I was a bowl,

capable of containing everything,

but then you revealed me

to be a strainer, a stranger to myself:

how dare I go around classifying myself

as an all-important container.

A strainer?

This means that you

filled holes in me

I never even knew existed.

These holes only became apparent

once you delisted from me,

and so,

the solution is obvious:

come back to me,

patch me up,

make me whole again.

These holes.

They get wider and deeper

every day.

And these holes.

They make me want you back

in the worst, worst way.

I want back

the way you wanted me.

We were symbiotic,

beautifully symbiotic.

I don't get it.

I don't get how you could stop.

It ended so abruptly,

without warning,

you didn't even give me

the chance to be ready.

And that made me wonder:

what is want?

Is it always fleeting?

Who is want?

Does it leave once it's satisfied?

Where does want go?

Is it to new lips,

new hands,

new bodies?

Do you remember how we met?

Do you remember how much

you wanted me

when we first met?

I do.

It is a moment

I can't seem to forget.

When I met you,

I wanted you

to notice me,

and not only that,

I wanted you to be

mesmerized by me,

because I was

hypnotized by you.

You were electric.

You sent lightning bolts

through me.

You were the first person

to set me on fire,

to awaken that thing –

that thing that all first loves awaken –

in me.

At that time,

I didn't have the words for it,

I just knew,

this was something unprecedented:

you would be a moment for me.

I want that moment again.

I want that honest, naïve,

unassuming, unguarded moment.

And I know

that was the old you,

but bring that you back,

please, just for a moment.

I want the old you back.

The you that knew me,

and the you that I knew.

I want to be able to

recognize your eyes again.

They're vacant now.

They hold nothing for me now,

and I can't understand it.

How?

Not long ago,

you would look at me

with desire and longing

and need and want.

Not long ago,

you would glance at me

and that glance would

turn into gaze,

and for no comprehensible

reasons at all,

your eyes would

follow me around endlessly.

But I always just figured

we must have been

thinking the same thing:

about how lucky we are

to want each other,

how lucky we are

to be this in want.

I want to breathe you in again.

Your scent is a rush to me.

It is danger and perilous

and overwhelming

in a way that I enjoyed.

And your scent,

it is the smell of inexpensive musk

and of stale herbs

and of crisp wood.

It is a scent that I will

always know as my first love,

and a scent that will instantly

break my heart when I

accidentally catch a whiff of it

elsewhere.

I want you to whisper

my name into my ear,

followed by all the things

the world beyond us doesn't know –

our jokes, our stories, our secrets.

These quiet thoughts float between us.

They belong to us.

I am yours,

and you are mine,

and they are ours.

And I want you

to brush your lips against mine

again and again,

gently, hello, hello,

never goodbye.

And I want you

to want to do these things.

Time is passing us by.

Each day that passes

is another day that

I have to be without you.

And I wonder...

aren't you wanting me too?

Judging by your

constant status updates

about how good it is to be free

(I didn't realize you were trapped) –

and your recent picture updates

featuring clubs you're going to now

(though when we were together,

you always told me you weren't into

all that…).

So I simply declare

that all of that is not true

and I tell myself that

deep down,

you're lonely too.

Deep down,

you must be

wanting me back, too.

Yet,

there's this constant nagging

on my back,

just as I step up to my

metaphorical mic.

And I realize:

I must be

what denial looks like.

Number Two: I Miss You.

I know you

inside outside inside,

and that is how you know me.

The only future

that I could ever see

is the one where

you would be

my co-lead.

Like in Hollywood,

I saw you running down the tarmac

to stop me

from getting on that plane.

Like in History,

I saw me sacrificing a nation

and inflicting pain,

waging war against our enemies

until they decreased.

Like in fairy tales,

I saw your beauty

calming my beast.

As it stands,

we have taken too much

of ourselves and

placed it into each other.

Like shoelaces,

we are interwoven,

unable to tie one

without the other.

Like a French braid,

intertwined,

so tightly,

knowing that necessity is

the thing that keeps us

from falling loose,

and apart,

stranded.

Like a gimp bracelet,

intersecting,

overlapping,

the elasticity of your love

gave me the freedom to be me.

With every fiber of my being,

I miss you.

And everything that you came with.

I miss the belonging-feeling.

And even though

you were possessive

and I was territorial,

and it was a mess,

we belonged to one another.

And even though

we were both jealous people,

and we would exhaust our lungs

shouting about insignificant things,

we were each other's problems.

And I long

to belong.

To you.

Again.

For we were also

each other's solutions.

We were perfectly placed,

perfectly disposed

to one another.

Our pieces fit

so well together,

not in the way that

puzzle pieces are

carved to click,

but in a clumsier,

more accidental way;

we were a city skyline –

unplanned architectural mastery.

Designed by the heavens,

and you called me your angel –

even when I was undeserving

of that accolade.

You'd call yourself the devil

and I'd feel betrayed.

Because for me,

we were the same,

either two sinners

or two saints.

I miss the reassuring-feeling.

When tiny thoughts of invalidity

would make their way

to the surface,

you silenced them.

You muted

my fears

and made my dreams

seem realistic.

Optimistic words

rushed out of your mouth

like a canoe down rapid rivers.

I never could criticize myself

in your presenc—

Hush-hush,

you reminded me

to speak softly of myself.

I miss the feeling of knowing.

I was sure of you.

I knew that

when I looked left,

you would be right there.

I was sure of you.

As sure as I was

as day would turn to night.

And, yes,

I've seen the moon

and the sun co-exist,

hanging,

for a single moment,

side by side.

Two of the most

opposite symbols

in the world

found peace,

so why can't we

figure it out

and find ease?

If this wasn't

meant to be,

I know I cannot force it.

Still, it is self-inflicted torture

the way that I

continue to hope

for a time around dawn,

when I the predictable sun

meet you the inconsistent moon.

I am determined.

I will stop missing you soon.

I have tried watching movies and cartoons.

I have tried hibernating and waiting.

I have tried exercising and gaming.

I have tried being with people and being alone.

Still,

missing you

is one of the greatest crises

I've ever known.

And that's how I learned

that every loss is not equal

just as every love is not.

Some shock,

others shake you to your core.

And the loss of you

shakes me

to my core.

I am lovesick.

How sick?

How cruel?

This feeling of

missing you.

Will it ever go for good?

Will there ever be a day

when I don't miss

the daylights out of you?

When physical distance

parted us,

I missed the physical things.

Yes, the hugs

and the kisses.

But, more so,

the soothing motion

of the tips of your fingers

running up and down my back,

and the playful brush

of your palm smacking

against my ass.

When it was physical distance

that separated us,

we would say,

I miss you,

I miss you,

I miss you,

so many times

it lost all meanings –

it became utterly diluted.

And now,

I would give anything

to return to those days

and hear you utter

that diluted phrase.

But when the distance

between us

wasn't this concrete,

tangible thing,

I should've known.

But…

I thought we were endless,

like the ocean,

like the sky,

like air.

And I am drowning

in a sea of my own tears

as I reach a quasi-acceptance.

I guess I accept that

you haven't

called,

texted,

or emailed.

I accept that maybe

it really is over.

But you are that one thing

that I have always counted on,

that one thing

that has kept me afloat –

you were my life jacket.

And I have cried enough tears

to fill my own ocean.

And there I go,

going under,

gasping for air

as my head

falls beneath the surface.

I am sinking.

The water is

pulling me down.

My body only begins to

feel heavier

when I try to hold it up

on my own.

Whoever said we were

weightless in water:

lied.

It's only once I

reach the very bottom

that I force myself

to stand up

because I have reached

a quasi-acceptance;

and even though

I miss you dearly,

I accept

that I have to

learn how to swim

on my own.

Number Three: You Moved On So Quickly.

There are two things

I hate about breakups:

the act of letting go

of someone

you've invested

so much time into

and the act

of moving on

from that person.

Some may argue

that this is the same act

because by letting go,

you're moving on,

or by moving on,

you're letting go.

But I disagree.

They're two different acts.

Two very different acts.

To me.

Letting go

is simply accepting that

something cannot be right now,

but maybe,

someday,

it'll come back

and everything will fall

into place.

But moving on is gettin' gone;

it is accepting that

something cannot be right.

Ever.

Ever, ever.

Ever, ever, ever.

And I don't know

which category

our situation falls into

(oh, please, be the first)

but—What's this?

What is this?

Who is this?

I can't believe

you moved on

so quickly.

Your New is

too short,

too skinny,

the hair is way too stringy.

It is too everything

that I am not.

But if I am no longer your type,

if you now like pears

and I am still an apple,

then you did not play fair

because you forgot

to let me know.

Like a blackout during the day,

I was in the dark

and I didn't even know.

So,

sure enough,

it doesn't take long

before New starts

marking territory.

Posting pictures,

and kissy faces,

and inside jokes.

I try again

to accept that

you have moved on

when I am nowhere near

ready to let you go.

Wanting to be

the good soldier,

I clench my teeth,

grin,

and bear it.

Knowing that I can't stop you

from sharing it,

I steel myself.

I am impenetrable.

But…

for those nights

when I'm up at 3AM,

and all my work's done,

and all my friends are asleep,

and I'm bored to death,

I will block you.

I will remove you.

I will delete you,

to stop myself

from checking in

on you

and New,

But one last time.

As I say goodbye to you

and your profile,

I can't fight

this feeling of exile.

I am an outlander.

And then.

I see it.

You and New

are celebrating your

one-month anniversary

for all of our friends to see –

only for me to see,

we've only been broken up

for two weeks.

Like a ton of bricks,

it hits me.

You were already there

before you had the cajones

to leave me.

I feel humiliated.

Words have always been

my strongest ally,

but in this moment,

I can no longer speak.

This is a new battle.

I need new artillery

because my old defense

cannot shield me

from this new pain.

Suddenly,

everything is a lie.

Every love you,

every want you,

every miss you.

I lie awake and think.

What happened to loyalty?

Did it come with a warranty?

Is loyalty only loyal to itself?

I was so foolish

to promise my forever to you.

Let go.

Forever isn't real.

Move on.

Forever isn't real.

But now I see you

promising forever

to someone new.

And I can't.

Out in the world,

I smile and carry on,

wondering if anyone can tell

I'm withdrawn.

When someone says your name,

I respond,

with a spurious, "who?"

Behind locked doors,

I crumble

because of you.

I shatter

into a thousand tiny pieces,

splintering myself

every time

I have to pick them up.

And every time

I have to put myself

back together again,

I wonder

how did humpty dumpty

survive this life?

Of course,

he didn't get stabbed by

a two-timing knife.

I yank that knife out of my back,

clench my teeth,

grin, and again,

I bear it.

I find solace in knowing

that someday you'll know

what it's like to wear it.

This shame.

This shock.

Of not being enough.

It's heavy.

I am burdened.

Make it stop.

Take it away.

I lie awake and think.

I am perplexed

by your sheer disrespect.

You replaced me.

It would've been one thing

if you had actually just

moved on from me.

That would've been painful enough.

But instead you—

you—

I can't even fathom you.

You took this sweet,

sacred love

and tossed it in the grinder.

Still,

I search high and low

for a reminder.

I justify you.

I justify the time

that we spent together –

you must have loved me more,

you must have given me more,

I get through nights believing

that I fought for someone

who'd fight for me.

I cannot tell you

the number of guys

I have compared you too,

but the thought to cross you

had never crossed my mind.

So, this comes

as a shock to my system,

and a joke to my mind.

You have made me

the punch line.

And you hit me

with your best shot.

You pain me.

It pains me

that you are still electric to me,

you still have that much

of an effect on me.

You send shockwaves

through me.

Shockingly enough,

I am still susceptible to you,

and it sucks.

Forget a thousand cuts,

you kill me with just one.

I can't be done.

I lie awake and think.

You not only moved on quickly,

you moved on

when you were still with me.

That is the mother of all betrayals.

The queen of all disrespects.

This has blind-sided me,

and it has brought me to my knees.

Please,

whatever I just said

about acceptance…

Forget that.

Like an eight-year-old,

I have to call psych.

Because I am no longer acceptance:

I am what rage looks like.

Number Four: I Hate You.

I never thought

I was capable of hate,

but I am.

And I hate you.

It dwells in my stomach.

It burns in my chest.

It sickens me.

You sicken me.

You are an incurable disease,

you are cancerous to me.

If forgiveness was the only way

to stay alive,

I would drop to death

hating you —

a happy demise.

Hatred haunts my dreams,

and hatred keeps me awake.

Sleep eludes me –

because now

I have to cross reference

every place you were ever at

when I wasn't there.

I have to think about

every private phone call

you ever took in the next room.

Because I don't know

if New was the only one.

All I know is,

I wasn't your only one.

And it makes me

so goddamn angry

that you put me

in this position,

having to listen to other people's

commentary:

about how

no self-respecting person would...

about how

they can always tell when…

about how

quickly they would move on to the next if…

Here I am:

The humiliated one,

because how could I not know?

There should've been signs.

Stop.

I am driving myself crazy.

There are no U-turns,

no turning this thing around,

you are a dead end to me now.

I can only go one way,

and that's why I speed toward hate.

Hate fuels the meanest part of me,

and I want that part

to be a part of me

for as long as possible.

I let it drive me.

I let it takeover.

If hate is my automatic

and default setting,

I don't have room for hurt

or sadness or angst.

Even though this hate

that I harbour for you

eats me up,

I don't even care.

It exhausts me,

it has me running on empty,

but I don't even care.

I said I don't even care, but

I begin to bargain.

What could I have done

more,

different,

or better?

What does New do

more,

different,

or better?

I wonder what it is

that you two do now

or did when we were together.

You and New must

sit around and laugh at me,

for I was the all too trusting fool

who fell victim to your love.

But as Doris Day

and my mother used to say

whatever will be, will be,

but reality check,

New hasn't got anything on me.

Anything,

anything to make this make sense.

And I hear it.

I know it.

I know I break New down

to build myself up,

but that's hate.

That's hating you,

hating New,

hating me.

How disrespectful you are.

How selfish you are.

How messed up you are.

And how these things

are becoming internalized by me.

It gets dark and cold in here.

The hate is deep in me,

pulsing through my veins,

it's all that remains.

I teeter on hate;

I am a seesaw.

And here we go again,

I go back and forth,

and back and forth,

and back and forth.

Every time I think

I have it figured out,

you yank

the rug out

from under me.

I catch wind of you

trying to tell people

I was crazy. Crazy? *Crazy?*

Deep breaths...

and one,

and two,

and three—

and you will rue the day

that you went and betrayed me.

Then you go and call New

your true first love.

Others might rise above,

but not me.

Not now.

You lie to them

or you lie to me,

but either way,

I see,

you're a lying liar who lies.

And I'm losing my head,

losing my cool,

losing the beautiful memories

I had of me and you.

My broken heart breaks again.

And I hate you so much that

I should be over you by now.

All that is said and done

in the name of love

is trickery.

You are a magician,

and I allowed you

to have your secrets.

I thought asking you

to reveal them

would've been

a sign of weakness.

In me.

In us.

You pulled flowers

from your sleeve

and promised me

you'd never leave.

But you performed

the greatest act of all,

I blinked

and you disappeared on me.

I carry the shame

of being your chains.

The handcuffs to your Houdini–

You escaped.

So,

you see,

I hate you.

I hate you

for making me feel genuine hatred.

I hate you

for making me question our time together.

I hate you

for choosing New.

I hate you

for making me hate myself.

I hate—that you don't even care

about any of this.

I can't let myself let go of this hate.

I'd rather stay vexed

because I don't know

what feelings are coming

to me next.

Number Five: I Am Lost.

I had been prepared

for all sorts of emotions,

but I hadn't

prepared myself

for nothingness.

I feel nothingness,

now.

The hate dissipated –

and after hate –

apparently,

evidently,

comes nothingness.

I am comforted

and contented by this,

and the feeling of contentment

surprises me.

I feel fully functional.

So,

I decide to go out

and see what it is you like

about these clubs so much.

The lights,

the music,

the vodka,

the people –

it makes you fade away.

No.

It makes you fly away.

With my feet off the ground,

I am superhero.

Invincible.

Untouchable.

I feel no pain,

no hate,

no anger,

no nothing.

And yet,

when I wake up

in the morning

with smeared makeup

and a dry throat,

I am still lost

and my heart is still broken.

A reminder,

a flicker of something

in my nothingness.

So,

night after night,

I go out and I fly.

I fly so high so

my thoughts never

have to revert back to you.

And it turns out,

I love to fly.

The takeoff is the best part.

It's something about the escape.

It's something about leaving

my lacklustre life behind,

if only for a little while.

It's like I'm not tied

to the earth anymore,

I'm not bogged down

by its burdens and heart aches.

As soon as I am off the ground,

soaring three thousand feet in the air,

through the clouds,

I am unconquerable.

And while I'm sky-high,

I sample

from the vast

selection of clouds.

Too thin,

too thick,

too rough,

too plush.

But finding all these new things

that don't suit me

show me the things that do.

I not only discover

for the first time,

with childlike wonder,

with awe,

I also rediscover

things about myself.

I am amazed at my reach.

My reach is greater

than I could've imagined.

I am an albatross.

I've grown wings,

wings that flap through winds,

and winds that carry me.

Wings and winds,

and this is freedom.

I never realized

I didn't feel free with you.

I never realized

I never inhaled with you.

Alone,

I have wings

flapping in the wind.

Flying is fun.

Remember

when we were together

and you used to outshine me

at every turn?

I hadn't minded it much.

That's who you were.

You always needed a spotlight,

always needed to be the centre

of attention. And I didn't.

Or at least,

I thought I didn't.

Somehow,

I was always pushed

to the outskirts

and the background,

an extra

in your life,

I lingered.

You wanted me

to live in your little shadows,

but that's no place

for a star.

You never demanded

that I shine.

Looking back,

I wonder if this

was an act of kindness,

allowing me to wallow

in my comfort zone

or if my inability

to stand centre stage

made you more important.

This flying thing

has taught me to dance

in the light,

the spotlight of centre stage.

I'm here, I cheer.

Lights up.

But flying…

is also…

draining.

There's an air of façade

I have to keep up.

I'm the life of the party now.

I'm the go-to for the good time.

It doesn't really matter

what my heart is

trying to say to me

beneath it all.

I shut it down.

I shut it off.

(For wasn't it this silly,

fallible organ that put me

in this position

in the first place?)

And I stay up,

not because I'm afraid to fall,

but because

despite the occasional fakery,

flying is still kind of fun.

So,

 on the days that I have to fake it,

I'll fake the fun.

I'm not coming undone,

I swear.

I just fly,

and move,

onward,

upward,

forward.

There's the occasional turbulence.

The realization

that I don't know

what you're doing now

or who you're doing it with.

I don't know where to find you

or how to contact you,

but it doesn't weigh on me.

I don't give much time

to consider it –

cause that's the thing

about this flying thing,

I'm doing it solo.

I'm finally doing it,

flying solo.

And although it's good to be a pilot,

I'm finding I'm out of touch.

I'm finding I'm just barely missing

these pitfalls,

these spirals,

these whirlpools.

And I'm finding this life,

spending every day

in the clouds,

is an aimless,

directionless,

wasteful life.

But I'm finding

the one thing I can't seem to find

is a safe place to land…

I am at war with myself.

Must a fighter pilot fly alone?

Like the perfect navigator,

like GPS,

one person recognizes

my lost-ness.

That person reaches for me.

That person brings me back down to earth.

That person tells me to fly

for the right reasons.

To the right places.

And just like that,

I remember who I am,

and mostly,

I am found.

Number Six: I Am Your Loss.

Yes, I am your loss,

and you are no longer mine.

After a period of time,

I realized this:

I would've followed you

into the deepest waters,

through the hottest deserts,

over a cliff,

into a snake pit —

because that is love.

Sometimes love

isn't patient or kind.

Sometimes it's rushed.

Sometimes it's late.

Like a hungry, caged lion

swiping its claws

through the gaps

between the bars:

Love is a jungle.

You called yourself a king,

and I liked that.

You identified with lions,

and I understood that.

I felt it made me queen,

a fierce feline.

Where I thought I was Nala

and you were Simba,

I forgot

you still shared

the bloodline of Scar,

a traitor.

You traitor.

And I remind myself:

You cheated

because you're selfish,

not because I wasn't enough.

You thought

there was enough of you

to be passed around,

and there wasn't.

I wouldn't call you empty.

If I were to call you empty,

what would that have made me

(your ex-other half)?

But I thought you were

the glass half-full,

turns out

when I turned around

I found

you were half empty.

I poured myself into you.

I gave more than I thought

was physically possible.

When the contents

of myself ran low,

I scraped the bottom

to give you more.

When the contents ran out,

I chipped at myself

giving you parts of me

I didn't have any business

giving away.

But you didn't hold the pieces

I was breaking myself

to give you sacred.

I really don't know

how I could've loved you.

I don't know how

I could've been so wrong

choosing you.

I don't know how

you could have had

the audacity to choose me!

It's almost insulting,

but perspective is altering.

It feels so good

to remove the

foggy goggles

and see you.

It is a fact that I am

slightly far-sighted.

That's probably the reason why

I never saw you

for who you really are,

and the reason why

when I scrutinized you

under a magnifying glass,

you didn't hold up—

it's perspective.

Perspective is like you,

perspective is a liar.

Your actions

had nothing to do with me.

My heart knows this now.

Because my heart has seen

the bottom of more soles

than a sidewalk

in New York.

And my heart has seen

the bottom of more souls

than a reaper who does this

kind of thing for work.

And oh,

you tried to leave me

for dead.

And oh,

I've got all the things

you last said

about who I would never be

and what I could never become

without you

bouncing around

in my head,

but I am purging you,

and after that,

I will never think of you again.

I am your loss.

You lucked out

the first time

you got me.

I will give you that.

It's just,

now I realize,

when I was with you,

it wasn't always

lollipops and daisies.

I did backflips and somersaults

to impress you,

and you wouldn't even

tumble for me.

More times than not,

I was waiting for the rain.

Like spring time.

Just before the flowers bloom.

Only we weren't buds first.

We skipped that part

and went straight to the part

that was supposed

to be beautiful.

The blossom.

Only, a blossomed flower

dies when the season changes.

Perhaps we needed to too.

That is the circle of things.

Seeing what the new season brings.

I am here, now,

finally seeing you

for who you truly are.

Perspective is a glimpse,

and the pit in my stomach shrinks.

Because you have made it

so much easier for me

to weed out

the fakes,

the hustlers,

the wannabes,

the never gonna-be's.

And I am your loss.

I treated you right.

I treated you with respect.

And as I purify

my thoughts of you,

I find pleasure

in knowing

you will never be able

to filter me out,

because I never

did anything

to damage you.

I have tussled

with this thing

called hindsight.

I am a better person

in spite of you.

You didn't make me good

(I thought you did).

You didn't make me whole

(I swear to God, I thought you did).

And I thought these things

'cause you implied them.

That is the flaw of you,

you have much work to do.

But – I don't think of you

every day anymore.

You don't consume me anymore,

and thank goodness for that.

The next time

someone consumes me,

I will make sure

they aren't rotten inside,

broken to the core,

garbage that penetrates

every single pore.

I see you now.

Everything you touch

turns to trash,

and that is why

I don't want your hands

on me anymore.

I'm reclaiming the pieces of me

I gave you to hold.

And I am your loss

because whereas

I gave you gold,

you gave me dust...

and trust

issues.

Number Seven: Love Is Different For Me Now.

I understand now

that all people have

two faces.

The one you can know

and the one you can't.

The demons you can know

and the ones that will

take you by surprise.

And I'll always have

to watch for it,

to search for it,

to wait for it.

Even then,

even on guard,

I know there's a possibility

I could miss it.

The reward

will always

have to feel

greater than

the risk.

Love is a game.

This is a sad truth.

I didn't want to be a player,

but love left me no choice.

Love requires a game plan.

Without one,

I'll lose.

Or be made to surrender.

Being the first one down,

or the first one out

is no longer a risk

I'm willing to take.

This isn't up for debate.

You were a pro

and you conned me,

so we don't need to

go back and forth on this.

This is a mistake

I can't make again.

I used to love hard.

Now, I look for easy.

This love comes with conditions,

now.

Now,

I keep score.

This love is limited,

now.

Now,

I can't do more

for love

than love does for me.

And now,

this love expires.

Love is different for me now.

So, I hope

when love comes to me again,

it doesn't come to me

like you did.

I hope it comes slowly.

In fact,

I hope love lives

on the other side

of the world

and has trouble catching

planes, trains, and boats

to get to me.

I hope love's car breaks down.

Fifty times.

At least.

I don't know

what love will look like

the next time it appears.

It could be better groomed,

it could have a weaker sense of humor,

it could be shorter than me.

I'm not excited to find out.

There is no rush.

Because all I can think about

is that this new love

will be like me,

it will be lugging luggage

from a previous love.

It won't be pure

and innocent

and unassuming.

It will be cautious.

And is cautious love

a love I want?

Love is different for me now.

Now, I am different.

I am scared.

For a while,

I was scared

that you would want me again

(I didn't know if

I would be able to say

no to you then),

but the fact of the matter is,

you don't know me anymore.

You can only know

the tiniest pieces

of what I allow you to see,

but I will never be

transparent to you again.

People tell me

that watching us

was like watching a bunny

get devoured by a wolf.

But wolves only belong one place –

in the wild.

You will never again

have the chance

to destroy me with that smile.

I will leave every bridge burned,

and every stone turned,

and you will never find

your way back to me.

I will crack every compass,

and cover my tracks,

and you will never

be able to find me.

You are a lost soul

and I am a True North,

and you will never

be able to find me.

Still I am scared.

I am scared

that love will never

be able to find me.

I am scared that

new will cheat on me too.

I am scared that

new will not fight hard enough for me.

I am scared that

new will find that the bricks that build

the walls around my heart

are too heavy

or that the deck

that new has been dealt

is defected;

it's missing a few key cards,

like the Queen of Hearts.

But mostly,

I'm scared

I won't recognize love again.

When love walks into the bar –

tall, dark, and handsome…

when love turns into my favourite aisle

at the grocery store –

searching for me,

I won't recognize it.

I'm scared that

even after love

identifies itself as love,

I won't believe it.

Even if I want to believe love –

there will be this invisible thing

between us,

whispering,

liar.

Love is different for me now,

and that's love's fault.

Love was romanticized.

Love was promised to me as good.

Who can I blame for this deception,

but the deceit-er?

Movies,

modern fairy tales,

and couples who stood the test of time

promised me a happy ending.

And it has felt like the end

many times.

For this,

love is to blame.

But – I am not happy yet,

so maybe,

this isn't the end.

It's one end,

but it isn't *The End.*

And yes,

love is so different now,

but it isn't gone.

It hasn't vanished entirely.

When you left,

it stayed behind.

It didn't stay for you though.

Love stayed for me.

Number Eight: Yes, I Am Over You.

But you finally called

and texted

and emailed.

Isn't that something?

I guess you heard about

the date that I went on last night.

When you asked how it was –

I lied.

It didn't go well.

It didn't go well

because I wasn't open enough.

I wouldn't take down

every brick of my wall

that you forced me to build.

I wouldn't show my date

every card in my deck

that you forced me to hide.

When I got home last night,

I cried.

It was the first time

in a long time

since our breakup

that I cried.

But this time,

I didn't cry over you.

I cried over the traces of you.

No matter where I would go,

no matter who I would be with –

traces of our wrecked love story

would always haunt

my future relationships.

We are a sunken ship

and there are no survivors.

We are the Flying Dutchman,

doomed to never make it to port,

fated to never make it work.

I am a ghost to you now.

You cannot affect me.

I get that now.

So, I will stay away from you.

I will be the water to your oil,

I will always rise above you.

I will be seventeenth century treasure

to your lazy pirate,

I will be unfindable.

And I will make you

stay away from me.

I will be the mouse

to your elephant,

I will always send you

running the other direction.

I will be the repellent

to your mosquito,

I will never be anything

but poisonous to you.

Not because of hate.

I don't hate you.

I don't even hate that I loved you.

I just know that I will never

want,

miss,

hate,

or love you,

ever again.

You get nothing from me.

That is why

I will stay away from you

like the brilliant stars

in the night sky

that never touch the earth.

The world is so vast.

I can see that now.

Now that I go weeks

without thinking of you –

months even,

and this place is beautiful.

This place is paradise.

I manifested paradise

on my own.

I don't carry

that dead love

I had for you

with me anymore.

I've got too many

other things to carry.

I've got my dignity,

my pride,

my self-respect,

and my self-love,

and these things,

they're a lot,

but they're light.

I am light as a feather

in comparison

to what I used to carry for you.

And where my first date

was a natural disaster,

my second and third

went by a lot faster.

We went to an exquisite

art exhibit

and I still felt like

the most beautiful thing

in the building.

Even though I didn't get a look

behind the scenes,

I realized

I didn't need too.

We only spoke about the future.

We went to an ice cream parlour,

and I was overwhelmed

by the number of flavours.

So many options.

So many choices.

I used to hate these moments –

because a choice

brought about your voice

in my head,

but out on this date…

it didn't.

You were gone.

This new place is peace.

When the hurting ceased,

And when I stopped looking,

Karma came around.

And I find it really funny

that you are trying

to come back to me now.

When you said

you were done with me,

it killed me.

You killed me.

Somehow,

I found a way

to live life at a ten.

I didn't resurrect

so you could do it again.

I stand alone now.

I am gravity,

I hold myself down now.

And I hold myself up.

It's last call at the bar,

but now,

I'm not stumbling out,

dazed and confused.

I'm strutting to my car,

and I see you from afar,

and it does nothing to me.

You.

I am over you

like the *do not break* seal

atop a glass container.

I used to think

that I would never

be a container again,

that the holes

you left in me

would never patch

themselves up,

but I was wrong.

How incredible,

how important it is

that I have learned

that I have the ability

to heal this way.

For a long time,

I couldn't look in the mirror.

I didn't want a reflection

that would show me how

broken I'd been.

But time went on.

The resilient sun

rose every morning.

It always had to face itself.

So I looked.

The person I saw

looking back at me

was unsightly –

but I recognized

myself instantly.

It is ironic to me that

the physical absence of you

pained me to no end

but the emotional absence of you

in me

is this endless relief.

And it took

a hell of a lot longer

than I thought it would.

But here I am.

Without you.

I am without you.

Number Nine: I Forgive You.

Even though

you never said sorry,

I forgive you.

Even though

you don't deserve it,

I forgive you.

Even though,

I can never love

another person

the way I did you –

completely,

and in total blind faith,

I forgive you.

Forgiveness isn't easy for me.

I used to falsely forgive you.

I would move

past hurtful words

knowing you would

speak them again,

and I would accept apologies

knowing in my insides

they were insincere.

False forgiveness

meant you would stay.

False forgiveness

meant I kept some anger at bay.

This isn't that.

I forgive myself, too.

I forgive myself for

settling for a love

that was finite, mediocre,

bounded, and conditional.

If love comes again,

it will come correct

because I won't settle

for anything less.

So, I forgive you.

I have stopped peeling,

and my scars have started healing,

and I have faith

that I will love again,

so I forgive you.

As a child,

I saw the women around me

break and bend for love.

They were warriors fallen,

when love came calling.

They boxed their inner warriors

and bowed to love's command.

These were the lessons,

even though they were unplanned.

I forgive them

for not realizing what

they didn't mean to teach me.

So here me when I say this:

I am full of forgiveness.

I am no longer

caught between

a compilation of dreams,

I just have my own.

And I know who I am

when I'm all alone.

In a way,

I think I've always

kind of known.

This is what has happened to me.

This is my latest epiphany.

People who were

so secure in themselves

used to frighten me.

How did they get to be that way?

Who gave them permission

to be so unreservedly themselves?

But I am getting there.

When you hear my name,

you will be in search of redemption.

You will want attention

and have confessions,

but please don't forget,

I am out of your dimension.

I am a rocket.

The world is my

giant launching pad.

When you hear my name,

you will be blown away.

I can recognize

that I'm not the old me,

I'm not who I used to be.

I no longer suffer

and I'm a tremendous amount tougher.

I learned to survive,

and not only that,

I learned to thrive.

The next time you hear my name,

it will be associated

with independence,

fearless independence.

I am reconciling

this newfound independence

with being independent

in a relationship.

I am a recovering romantic.

Nine steps later.

I am running.

I see the finish line of this,

and the potential start

of a new race.

And that is part of the reason

why I am full of forgiveness.

The next time I meet someone,

I will not go into it

with naïve assumptions.

I will not treat it

as a one hundred metre dash,

I will see the marathon.

Somehow,

somehow,

yet again,

I will be love's fool.

I am willing to offer myself up

to love on a platter.

A vet on the matter,

I now understand the power

I can give someone to hurt me…

but I will probably hand it over anyway.

I find myself,

slowly,

finally,

reattaching the hopeless to the romantic.

With new understanding.

With new reservations.

Because I also understand now

that people damage people.

People damage people,

sometimes without realizing,

sometimes without regret,

but never without the possibility of repair.

I understand that now.

I think that's why love

is both beautiful and tragic

and beautifully tragic.

I currently live by the motto

'all love ends in tragedy.'

Because it does:

distance, despair, damage or death.

Yet, that will not stop me

from chasing love,

or from finding the person

who is supposedly meant to be

the person that's for me –

the person that is supposedly

supposed to fit into the spaces

between my fingers,

and fit into the length of my arms,

and fit into the crevices of my body.

And I have to keep my head up

because I know,

somewhere out there

is the person that's for me,

walking around,

waiting for me to arrive.

I just know.

And even though

all love ends in tragedy,

I believe in reaping what we sow.

And, with that being said,

I will gladly wait

for my next tragic Romeo.

In truth,

I have given this heartbreak

too much time and attention.

In truth,

I may have made this

moment in my life overly significant.

In truth,

this journey is not

a heroic one.

It does not concern

nations or cultures.

I am not a butterfly

who flaps its wings

and causes a tornado.

In truth,

millions of people before me

have experienced heart aches

a thousand times worse than mine

and millions of people

yet to be born

will know heart ache

a thousand times greater.

And that isn't perspective,

that is truth.

And I forgive you

because the truth is,

I'm breathing.

I'm good.

I'm better.

So,

as I begin

to step back

from this

metaphorical mic,

get a good look

at me

because I am what

forgiveness

looks like.

Number Ten: Goodbye.

I am caught off guard

by the lump

lodged in my throat.

I don't want to cry.

I won't cry.

I don't even actually need too.

The lump is from discomfort.

And discomfort is what we feel

when we must do what we must.

I must say goodbye to you.

I've tried

to do this a million times already,

before I was truly ready.

Even though I am

currently having a hard time

putting the good in front of the bye,

I am ready

to bid you adieu.

To recap.

You were my first forever.

A first forever,

a first love,

must be chosen wisely,

but nobody ever uses

first love and wise

in the same sentence.

Or first love and choose,

for that matter.

It turns out that

I wasn't my first love's first love.

I don't know how

I missed the lesson in that one.

You were my first love,

and then you were a burden to me.

And then you were nothing.

And now you're a memory.

Memories are changing.

At first, our memories

were a comfort to me.

They were the hug I needed

when your arms abandoned me.

But then these memories

became a reminder that our love

wasn't what I thought it was,

and the memories taunted me.

Now, they are just memories.

There's no emotional value

attached to them.

So...

maybe the memories don't change,

but the feelings do.

The feelings have changed

and changed again,

and I have said goodbye to those feelings.

You can't say goodbye to memories.

(I will be sure

to be careful

about who I make

future memories with.)

I had wondered endlessly

if it would be possible

to say goodbye to you.

I thought you would

always be a part of me,

but you are not.

You are completely

out of my system.

The things I loved

because you loved them are gone,

or are replaced with my own reasons

for loving them.

I don't remember

or even want to remember

the taste of your lips anymore.

– *Goodbye.*

There it is.

I am ready to go now,

more than ready.

And yet,

there's something sad

about a true ending.

Like death,

I put you in your coffin,

and bury you,

and even if I visit you

at your grave site,

there is no way for us to reconnect.

Goodbye, goodbye.

There's no room for me

down there.

Goodbye.

Our time together

is a message in a bottle,

captured and contained,

beautiful and lost at sea.

The more time it spends there,

the more the lines on the pages' fade;

It's not meant to be found.

Goodbye, goodbye,

I carry no ill will for you.

My hopes for you are abundant.

I hope

all your wildest dreams come true.

I hope

you know love that is tremendous

and extraordinary.

I hope

you know so much joy

that you feel you could die of it

with no regrets.

But if your dreams don't come true

or you never know love again,

or you don't find happiness,

it's no great concern of mine.

Goodbye, goodbye, goodbye.

When all my fears

about who I would become

dissolved,

I realized

that with this new growth

and sense of self,

I could afford to be

fifty percent of a couple

without being half of a whole.

Goodbye, goodbye.

My soul

made a decision about you

a long time ago.

It believed in you.

It loved you.

Even with the unconscious knowledge

that you weren't its true mate.

Goodbye.

I'm now focussed

on my second forever.

A forever

I haven't been introduced to yet,

but one that comes with

so much potential,

and one that I am ready

to invest boundless energy in.

Whereas I used to be like a candle,

carrying a light

that would eventually

run low and diminish,

burning itself to the ground,

I now carry a light

that never dies.

If future love interests

try to dim me,

they will not succeed.

I have learned.

I have decided

I will be foolishly cautious,

foolish and cautious

with my future love interest.

And I won't love weakly.

And I won't blame

my future love interests

for things that were us.

And I won't mistake

romance and relationship.

And I have decided

I am easy to love.

But these are the start of my vows

to a future love,

and they don't concern you...

because you are no longer mine, love.

No longer my love.

And suddenly,

this goodbye

feels like the easiest thing

I've ever done.

Good and bye.

Goodbye to you,

my first failed forever.

Goodbye to you,

my first ex.

And with nothing

left to say to you,

Goodbye.

Signed,

Your Ex

Fin.

ABOUT THE AUTHOR

Bianca Perrie was born in Toronto, Canada. She holds a Bachelor of Arts degree in English Literature and a Bachelor of Education degree. When she's not writing about love, she's reading romantic novels, watching romantic movies and/or binging any TV series with a will-they-won't-they couple. Her other faves include coffee, wine, chocolate, and puppies.

MORE BOOKS BY BIANCA PERRIE

Printed in Great Britain
by Amazon

84294918R00073